A RIVER JOURNEY

The Nile

Rob Bowden

HODDER
Wayland

an imprint of Hodder Children's Books

A RIVER JOURNEY

The Amazon	The Ganges
The Mississippi	The Nile
The Rhine	The Yangtze

A River Journey: The Nile

Text copyright © 2003 Rob Bowden
Series copyright © 2003 Hodder Wayland
First published in 2003 by Hodder Wayland,
an imprint of Hodder Children's Books.
Reprinted in 2004

Commissioning Editor: Victoria Brooker   Designer: Jane Hawkins   Cover design: Hodder Wayland
Book Editor: Debbie Fox   Picture Research: Shelley Noronha, Glass Onion Pictures
Book consultant: Professor Tony Allan   Maps: Tony Fleetwood
Series consultant: Rob Bowden,   Cover Design: Hodder Wayland

Series concept by: Environment and Society International –
Educational Resourcing

British Library Cataloguing in Publication Data
Bowden, Rob
 Nile. - (A river journey)
 1. Nile River - Juvenile literature 2. Nile River - Geography
 - Juvenile literature
 I. Title
 916.2

ISBN 0750240415

Printed in China

Hodder Children's Books
A division of Hodder Headline Limited
338 Euston Road, London NW1 3BH

Picture Acknowledgements

Cover James Davis; 1 Hodder Wayland Picture Library; 2, 5 Rob Bowden; 6 Andes Press Agency/Carlos Reyes-Manzo; 7 Bridgeman Art Library/Royal Geographical Society, London,UK; 8 T de Salis/Still Pictures; 9 (left) Caroline Penn/Impact; 9 (right), 10, 11 Rob Bowden; 12 Mark Deeble & Victoria Stone/Oxford Scientific Films; 13 (top) Joan Root/Oxford Scientific Films, (bottom) Fred Hoogervorst/Panos Pictures; 14 Richard Kemp/SAL/Oxford Scientific Films; 15 Robert Harding Picture Library; 16 (top) Art Wolfe/Science Photo Library; (bottom) G.Verhaegen/Still Pictures; 17 (top) Katri Burri/Panos Pictures, (bottom) Robert Harding Picture Library; 18 Trip/H Rogers; 19 Paul Almasy/Corbis; 20 Travel Ink/David Forman; 21 Topham; 22 NASA/Science Photo Library; 23 (top) Hutchison Picture Library, (bottom left) Trip/H Rogers, (bottom right) Impact?; 24 Colin Jones/Impact; 25, 26 Colin Jones/Impact; 27 (top) Toby Adamson/Still Pictures, (bottom) Eyal Bartov/Oxford Scientific Films; 28 Rob Bowden; 29 (top) Popperfoto, (bottom) Alex Dufort/Impact, (bottom right) Toby Adamson/Still Pictures; 30 Eye Ubiquitous/Julia Waterlow; 31 Peter Kingsford/Eye Ubiquitous; 32 (inset) Rob Bowden, (bottom) and 33 Peter Kingsford/Eye Ubiquitous; 34, 35, 36 Julia Waterlow/Eye Ubiquitous; 37 (top) David Keith Jones/Images of Africa, (bottom) Bojan Brecelj/Corbis; 38 Rob Bowden; 39 (top) Ecoscene/Mark Carey, (bottom) Impact?; 40 Earth Satellite Corporation/Science Photo Library; 41 (top) Julia Waterlow/Eye Ubiquitous, (bottom) Bojan Brecelj/Still Pictures; 42 Hodder Wayland Picture Library; 43 Eye Ubiquitous/Steve Lindridge; 44 Gary John Norman/Panos Pictures

The maps in this book use a conical projection, and so the indicator for North on the main map is only approximate.

Contents

1: The source of the Nile — 6

HISTORY	Explorers of the Nile	7
NATURE	The true source	7
$ ECONOMY	Multi-purpose source	8
CHANGE	The future of the Falls	8
NATURE	A beautiful weed!	10
PEOPLE	The Basoga	11
NATURE	Into the Rift Valley	12
NATURE	Murchison Falls	12
$ ECONOMY	National Parks	13

2: Calming the Nile — 14

PEOPLE	The Dinka Pastoralists	15
NATURE	The great barrier	16
CHANGE	The Jonglei Canal	17

3: The rivers meet — 18

$ ECONOMY	The Gezira project	19
NATURE	Salinisation	19
NATURE	The Nile's big brother	20
PEOPLE	A spiritual beginning	21
$ ECONOMY	Using the Nile	21
NATURE	The Nile confluence	22
PEOPLE	Whirling Dervishes	23
HISTORY	The slave trade	23

4: The Nile Cataracts — 24

HISTORY	The Kingdom of Kush	25
NATURE	The Nile's little brother	25
PEOPLE	The Nubians today	26
NATURE	Ships of the desert	26
NATURE	The six cataracts	28
HISTORY	Abu Simbel	28
CHANGE	Aswan High Dam	29

5: The Nile Valley — 30

$ ECONOMY	Aswan	31
NATURE	Elephantine Island	31
$ ECONOMY	Tourism	32
HISTORY	Quarrying on the Nile	33
PEOPLE	The Fellahin	34
HISTORY	Luxor	35
$ ECONOMY	Cash cropping	36
HISTORY	Early paper	36
PEOPLE	Bustling riverbanks	37
HISTORY	The Pyramids of Giza	38
PEOPLE	A crowded city	38
NATURE	Air pollution	39

6: The Nile Delta — 40

$ ECONOMY	The delta farms	41
CHANGE	Greening the desert	41
NATURE	Impacts of Aswan	42
$ ECONOMY	Trade & shipping	43
PEOPLE	How many people?	44
CHANGE	Global warming	44

FURTHER INFORMATION	46
GLOSSARY	47
INDEX	48

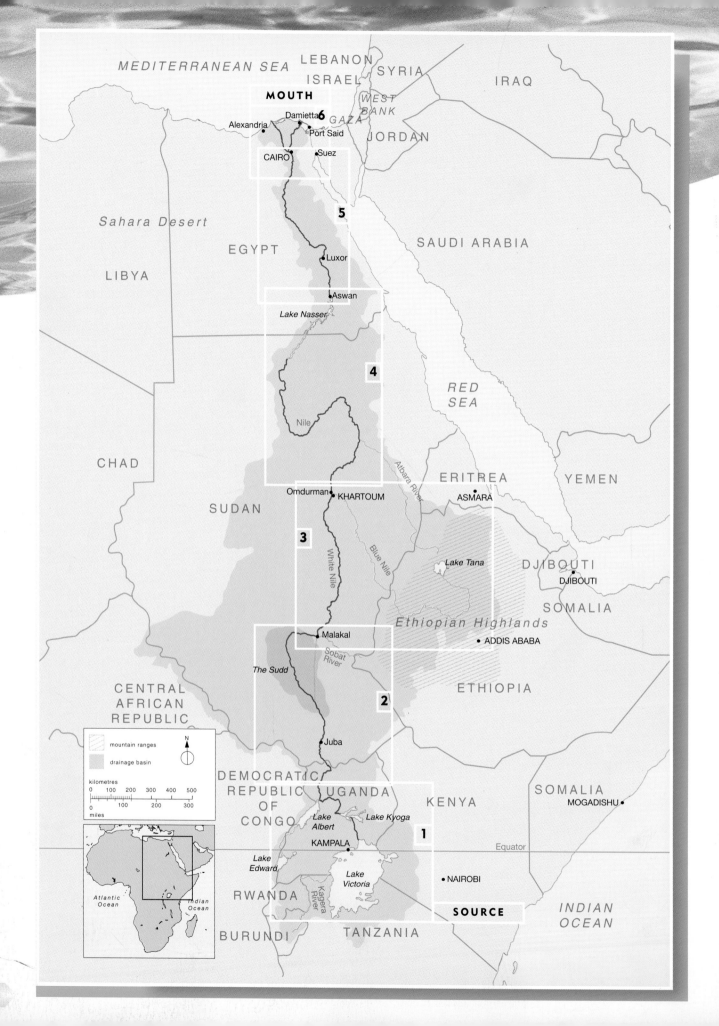

MEDITERRANEAN SEA
LEBANON
ISRAEL
SYRIA
IRAQ
WEST BANK
GAZA
JORDAN

MOUTH

Alexandria
Damietta **6**
Port Said
CAIRO
Suez

Sahara Desert

5

LIBYA

EGYPT

Luxor

SAUDI ARABIA

Aswan

Lake Nasser

4

RED SEA

CHAD

Nile

ERITREA

ASMARA

YEMEN

SUDAN

Omdurman
KHARTOUM

Atbara River

3

DJIBOUTI

Lake Tana

DJIBOUTI

White Nile

Blue Nile

SOMALIA

Ethiopian Highlands

Malakal

ADDIS ABABA

Sobat River

The Sudd

CENTRAL
AFRICAN
REPUBLIC

2

ETHIOPIA

Juba

mountain ranges

N

drainage basin

kilometres
0   100   200   300   400   500
0   100   200   300
miles

DEMOCRATIC
REPUBLIC
OF
CONGO

UGANDA

KENYA

SOMALIA

MOGADISHU

Lake Albert

Lake Kyoga

1

*Atlantic
Ocean*

*Indian
Ocean*

KAMPALA

Equator

*Lake
Edward*

*Lake
Victoria*

Kagera River

NAIROBI

RWANDA

SOURCE

BURUNDI

TANZANIA

*INDIAN
OCEAN*

Your Guide to the River

USING THEMED TEXT As you make your journey down the Nile you will find topic headings about that area of the river. These symbols show what the text is about.

🐇 **NATURE**   Plants, wildlife and the environment

📖 **HISTORY**   Events and people in the past

✋ **PEOPLE**   The lives and culture of local people

➡️ **CHANGE**   Things that have altered the area

💲 **ECONOMY**   Jobs and industry in the area

USING MAP REFERENCES   Each chapter has a map that shows the section of the river we are visiting. The numbered boxes show exactly where a place of interest is located.

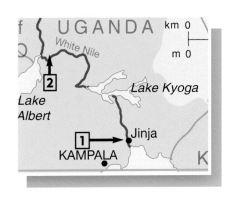

The Journey Ahead

We begin our journey where the White Nile leaves Lake Victoria, an enormous lake in the heart of East Africa. The calm waters of the lake form breathtaking rapids before slowing down in the swamps of Lake Kyoga. The Nile river then cascades over Murchison Falls into Lake Albert and tumbles through the rugged mountains of southern Sudan. As it leaves the mountains it meets the giant swamps of the Sudd, where it loses almost half its water.

In the twin cities of Khartoum and Omdurman, the White Nile is joined by the Blue Nile. Now a single river, the Nile is joined by the Atbara river. Then it heads north into Egypt and Lake Nasser, behind the Aswan High Dam. Below the dam, the Nile provides a narrow ribbon of life through the harsh deserts of Egypt. It passes ancient temples and the famous pyramids before reaching Cairo, one of Africa's greatest cities.

North of Cairo the Nile spreads out into a giant fan-shaped delta. It finally enters the Mediterranean Sea at the end of its incredible 6,670 kilometre journey.

As we travel along the Nile we will learn more about the people and places that line this extraordinary river.

Let's board a dhow to begin our journey. We'll take a short boat trip on Lake Victoria to the source of the Nile!

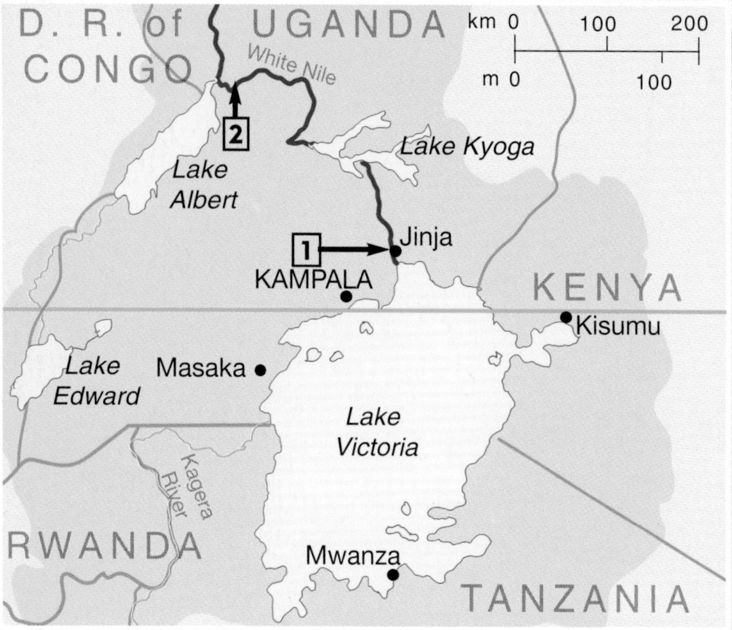
D. R. of CONGO
UGANDA
White Nile
km 0 100 200
m 0 100
2
Lake Kyoga
Lake Albert
1
Jinja
KAMPALA
KENYA
Kisumu
Lake Edward
Masaka
Lake Victoria
Kagera River
RWANDA
Mwanza
TANZANIA

1. The Source of the Nile

LAKE VICTORIA IS AFRICA'S biggest lake. It is surrounded by three countries – Kenya, Tanzania and Uganda – and is an important resource for the people who live on its shore. Near the town of Jinja on the northern edge of the lake, water pours over a waterfall into a narrow opening, and the Nile River is born. The waterfall, called Ripon Falls, is now submerged behind the Owen Falls Dam a little further downstream.

Below: This tree marks the source of the White Nile at Ripon Falls.

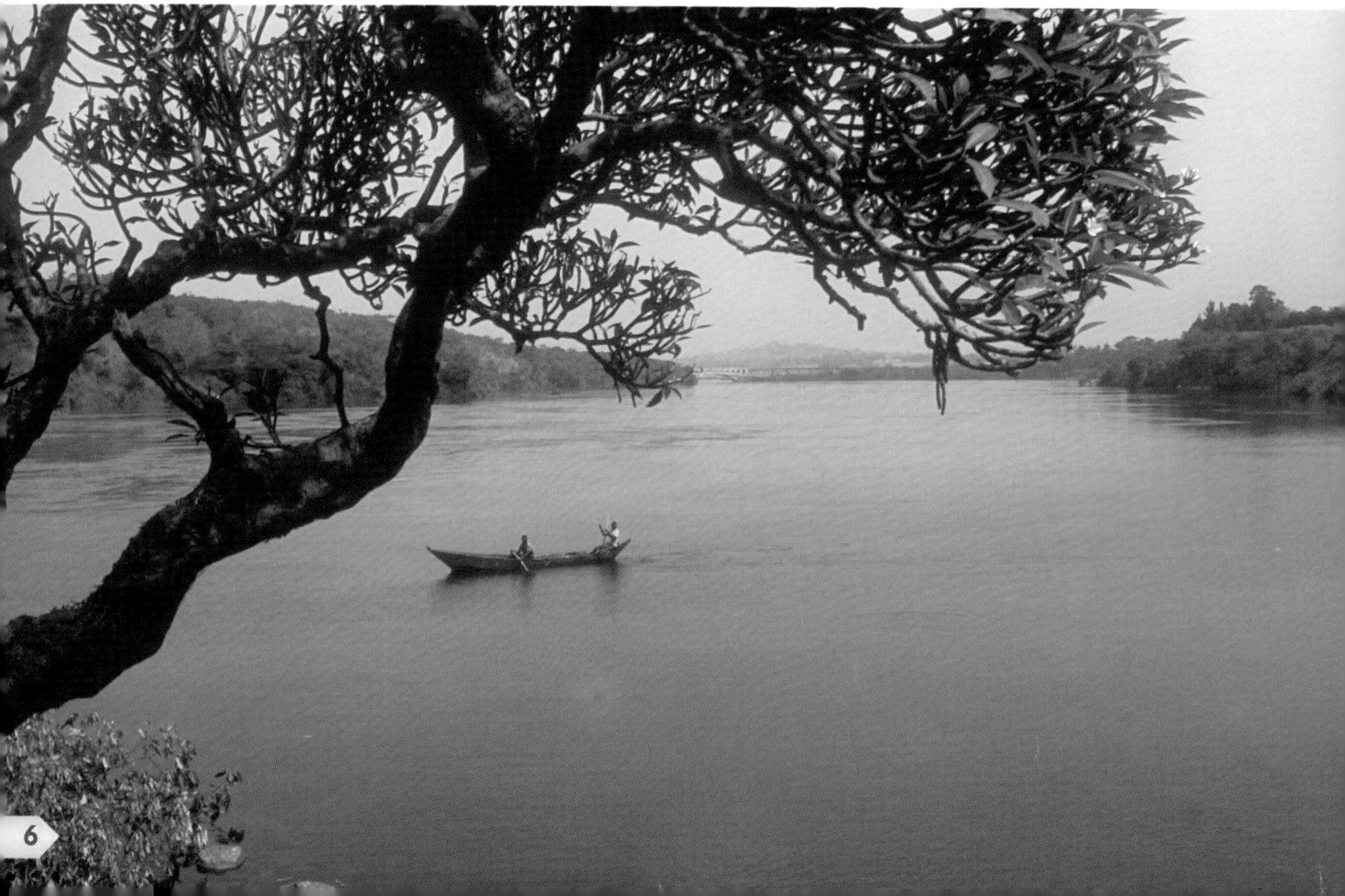

📖 HISTORY *Explorers of the Nile*

In 1857 two British explorers, Richard Burton and John Hannington Speke, left the East African coast to look for the source of the Nile. After many months they reached Lake Tanganyika, which Burton thought was the source. But Arab traders told them about an even bigger lake called 'Nyanza' and Speke thought that this must be the real source.

By this time Burton was too ill to continue, but Speke carried on alone. On 3 August 1858, he discovered a giant lake near Mwanza in what is now known as Tanzania. He declared this lake to be the source of the Nile and named it Lake Victoria after the British queen of the time.

Burton disagreed with Speke and so, in 1860, Speke organized another expedition to prove he was right. After two years of walking he finally came across a magnificent set of falls that he felt sure were the start of the Nile. Speke named them Ripon Falls and returned to London a hero. Burton still didn't believe him and challenged Speke to prove his discovery, but the day before their debate Speke died in a hunting accident.

The mystery continued to fascinate explorers until an American journalist called Henry Stanley sailed around the whole of Lake Victoria in 1875. He proved that Ripon Falls were indeed the source of the Nile. Speke was right after all.

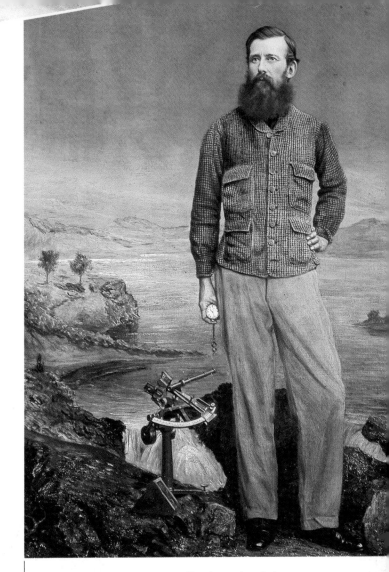

Above: John Hannington Speke solved the mystery of the source of the Nile in 1858.

🐰 NATURE *The true source*

Ripon Falls may be the starting-point of the Nile, but any streams that flow into Lake Victoria could claim to be the true source.

Streams tumble down from a chain of mountains that cross central Africa and surround much of Lake Victoria. The Kagera river and its tributary the Ruvubu with its headwaters in Burundi are now considered the true source of the Nile. It is from here that the Nile is measured as the world's longest river.

$ ECONOMY   *Multi-purpose source*

Within sight of the flooded Ripon Falls, the thick wall of Owen Falls Dam holds back the force of the Nile's waters. The power of the water turns turbines, which generate electricity as they spin round. This is called hydroelectric power (HEP).

An extension to the dam was opened in 2000 to meet Uganda's growing demand for electricity. Power shortages remain a problem, however, and only five per cent of Ugandans have any electricity at all. One solution would be to build more HEP dams across the Nile, but the river has other purposes too.

Just below Owen Falls Dam, the Nile's waters turn frothy and wild as they crash over a series of drops and rocks. This white water is some of the best in the world. It attracts thousands of adventure tourists who come to shoot the rapids in inflatable rafts, or canoes if they are really brave! We stick to the safer raft, but we still have to get over the Bujagali Falls ahead!

➡ CHANGE   *The future of the Falls*

Bujagali Falls MAP REF: 1 are one of Uganda's greatest natural treasures. They attract thousands of foreign and local visitors. The tourists come to watch the Nile as it surges past them in angry twists and turns. They can see the amazing variety of birds that live in the area, or shoot one of the best sets of rapids in the world. But the future of Bujagali Falls is threatened by plans to build a new HEP dam across the river.

> Below: The Owen Falls Dam was built in 1954. It transforms the power of the Nile into electricity for Uganda and its neighbour, Kenya.

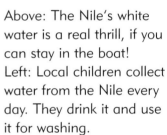

Above: The Nile's white water is a real thrill, if you can stay in the boat!
Left: Local children collect water from the Nile every day. They drink it and use it for washing.

Supporters of the scheme say the new dam will double the electricity generated by the Nile's waters. It will provide much-needed jobs and electricity for the Ugandan economy. Those against the dam say it will destroy a valuable tourist attraction and one of the country's most beautiful sites. They also say it will ruin the livelihoods of 7,000 local people – many more than the number who will have temporary jobs during the dam's construction.

Despite these concerns, it looks as though the Ugandan government will allow the dam at Bujagali to go ahead. If that happens, we could be some of the last people to see this amazing natural wonder.

Above: Water hyacinth look pretty, but they disrupt the fishing sites around Lake Victoria. Fishing nets can be ruined by this weed. It can take hours to untangle them.

NATURE A *beautiful weed*!

Water hyacinth is one of the biggest problems facing the Nile region. Although it is beautiful, it is also a destructive weed.

Once it is introduced to the water it grows rapidly. It can double in size in just six to fifteen days. Soon the water hyacinth creates thick mats that block sunlight and starve the water of oxygen. Fish and other plant life suffer or die. Fishing becomes impossible in some places, and water transport is severely disrupted. The weed even threatens electricity generation by blocking the turbines at Owen Falls Dam. Special dredging equipment can remove the hyacinth, but it is dangerous work as snakes and crocodiles live amongst the weed.

In 1993 a weevil that feeds on water hyacinth was introduced into Lake Kyoga to tackle the problem. Three years later it was released into Lake Victoria. This method of biological control seems to be working, but the weed still covers large sections of the river and lakes. New schemes to tackle the weed are now underway. They include plans to harvest it for animal feed.

PEOPLE *The Basoga*

The people we meet who live along this stretch of the Nile, between Lake Victoria and Lake Kyoga, are the Basoga. The Basoga are one of the largest ethnic groups in Uganda. They make up almost eight per cent of the total population.

The Basoga live in family groups and are mainly farmers. They use land given to them by a clan-head called the 'Mutaka'. They are subsistence farmers, and so almost all the food they grow is for their own needs. The fertile soil of the area allows them to grow a wide variety of crops, including bananas, millet, maize, beans, and vegetables. Coffee and sugar cane are also grown as cash crops. These are sold instead of being used by the family. The land closest to the Nile and the lake shores is considered the best because it is well watered. There, farmers can grow up to three crops a year.

Population growth means that the Basoga people are running short of land for farming. Many have therefore started fishing in the Nile and its lakes. This is an alternative way for them to earn money and supply food for their families. Men and older boys fish. The women and girls help with the cleaning, sorting, drying and selling of fish.

Below: Basoga women wash and sort fish. Some they will dry and keep, others they will take to the local market.

Left: The Nile creates fantastic plumes of spray as it crashes over Murchison Falls and into the African Rift Valley.

 NATURE **Into the Rift Valley**

As we leave Lake Kyoga behind us, we follow the river west. It drops several hundred metres over more rapids and waterfalls on its journey towards the western edge of the African Rift Valley. This giant valley stretches for 6,500 kilometres across East Africa and beyond. It is one of the few natural features on Earth that is clearly visible from space.

The Rift Valley was formed by the cracking and movement of the Earth's surface along lines known as faults. In some places the cracks allowed hot lava to escape, which formed volcanoes, and in others the land sank to form valleys.

NATURE **Murchison Falls**

The Nile crashes into the Rift Valley over the spectacular Murchison Falls [MAP REF: 2]. The river is forced into a narrow seven-metre gap, where it gains terrific speed before suddenly falling forty metres and landing with a deafening roar and plumes of spray below.

The falls developed where the power of the river cut away soft rock and created a drop. Over time the drop became higher and higher, as more soft rock was worn away. The local name for the falls is 'Bajao', which means 'devil's place'. They are too dangerous to paddle down so we must walk around them by land and board another boat on the far side.

$ ECONOMY *National Parks*

Murchison Falls National Park is a popular tourist site thanks to the double attraction of the falls and the wildlife living around them. We can see lions, elephants, giraffes and buffalo here, but the area really comes to life when we board a river launch to the base of the falls.

The river swells with hippos in their hundreds, and the riverbanks are lined with Nile crocodiles. Along much of the Nile, crocodiles have been almost wiped out by local people, who want to prevent their livestock (and themselves) from being eaten. So this is our best chance to see them on our journey. Keep your eyes peeled

Above: Hippos wallow in the Nile below Murchison Falls. The water keeps them cool in the hot tropical sun! In the evening hippos leave the water to graze on nearby land. They often destroy crops and there is an ongoing struggle between the hippos and local farmers as they compete to use the same land.

for the really big ones. A fully-grown crocodile can be over six metres long and can weigh over 700 kilograms!

The park is in one of the poorest parts of Uganda. The money tourists spend on visiting the falls and wildlife provides local people with an important source of income. Not everyone benefits though, and the luxury tourist camps are a world apart from most of the nearby villages.

We continue in our river launch until we cross into the country of Sudan.

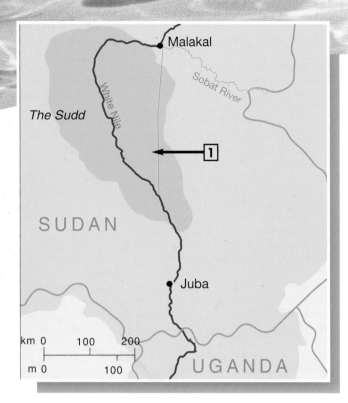

The Sudd

Malakal

Sobat River

White Nile

1

SUDAN

Juba

km 0   100   200

m 0   100

UGANDA

2. Calming the Nile

SHORTLY AFTER MURCHISON FALLS the Nile flows through the deep waters of Lake Albert before emerging from the north of the lake and heading towards the Uganda-Sudan border. The river here is wider and slower, but this calm is interrupted as we cross into Sudan. This stretch is called 'Al-Jabal', which means 'Mountain Nile'. Over the next 193 kilometres the river passes through narrow mountain gorges and crashes over yet more rapids. Streams from the surrounding mountains join the swirling, rushing waters and make the Al-Jabal too dangerous to navigate. We fly over this region and join the Nile again at Juba, just before the giant swamps of the Sudd.

Below: Dinka fishermen use spears to catch fish. The fish come closer to the surface of the water at dusk.

PEOPLE The Dinka Pastoralists

Juba is the main city of southern Sudan – an area inhabited by the Dinka people. The Dinka are pastoralists, which means they gain most of their livelihood by breeding and raising livestock. Cattle are especially important and form the centre of the Dinka's social and economic system. A man's wealth is judged by the number of cattle he owns; cattle are rarely killed because of their value. Instead, they are used for their milk or for trading. Even their dung is valued. It is dried for use as a fuel, or burned to make smoke to keep away mosquitoes.

Dinka men and boys as young as eight years old look after the cattle, guiding them to water and fresh pastures. During the rainy season the pastures are plentiful, but during the dry season the cattle are moved to the better-watered pastures near the Nile.

Above: Dinka boys bring their cattle to the river to drink. Here they graze on the lush vegetation along the riverbank.

Wild animals such as wildebeest and gazelle also migrate towards the river during the dry season. The Dinka have become skilled at hunting them, to provide meat and hides for clothing or sleep mats. They also catch fish from the Nile, which the Dinka women preserve by drying or smoking – there are no fridges here!

The Dinka are expert managers of their environment and the River Nile that flows through the heart of it. Unfortunately, Sudan's long civil war, which started in 1955, has severely affected them. Villages have been destroyed, people and livestock killed, and many traditional pastures are no longer safe to use.

Above: This African fish eagle is flying off with its catch in its claws.
Left: A Shoebill stork in front of papyrus reeds. Shoebills stand more than a metre high.

 NATURE *The great barrier*

North of Juba we notice a sudden change in the Nile as it levels off to a very shallow gradient. In fact, by this point, the Nile has completed over three-quarters of its descent, even though we are less than halfway through our journey.

The shallow gradient means that, during the rainy season, there is too much water for the Nile to carry. The river floods over the surrounding land. Marshy grasses and sedges including papyrus grow rapidly in these conditions. They form clumps that divert, block and spread the Nile's water over an enormous area known as the Sudd, meaning 'barrier'. The Sudd can be up to 320 kilometres long and 240 kilometres wide, which makes it

Right: The enormous bucketwheel carved the channel for the Jonglei Canal.

one of the biggest wetlands in the world. The area is famous for its birdlife, which includes kingfishers, storks and eagles.

The Sudd is important in regulating the flow of the Nile. It acts like a giant sponge, soaking up excess water during the rains. Then it gradually releases the water back into the river during the dry season. About half the Nile's water is lost, however, as it seeps into the soil or evaporates in the hot tropical sun.

→ CHANGE *The Jonglei Canal*

As the populations of Sudan and Egypt have grown, so have their demands for water. In the 1970s the two countries developed an ambitious plan to use the water that normally evaporated in the swamps of the Sudd. A 360 kilometre channel was planned to bypass the Sudd **MAP REF: 1**. This

would provide more water for people living downstream and reduce the journey between Juba and Khartoum by 300 kilometres.

Digging began in 1978 using a specially constructed machine called 'the bucketwheel', but work was halted in 1984 because of Sudan's civil war.

Two hundred and sixty-seven kilometres had been finished and the project was only a year away from completion. But there were signs that the impact on the environment, and on local Dinka people, would have been negative. Wetlands and pastures would have been drained, and migration routes for the Dinka and their cattle would have been disrupted. Whether the Jonglei Canal will ever be completed is uncertain.

We paddle through a clearing in the swamps of the Sudd as we continue our journey.

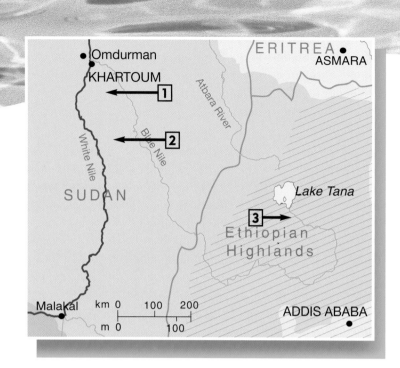

3. The rivers meet

NORTH OF THE SUDD the Nile is joined by its major tributaries. First the Sobat, which rises in Ethiopia (it is called the Bora river there). It replaces most of the water lost by evaporation in the Sudd. The Sobat joins the Nile near Malakal.

From here the White Nile broadens into a slow-moving channel, fringed with swampy plants. This channel continues for nearly 500 kilometres, until the Blue Nile comes racing down from the Ethiopian Highlands. It meets the White Nile in the twin cities of Khartoum and Omdurman. It is from this point that we can, at last, call the river simply, the Nile.

Below: Here cotton is being harvested. It is one of Sudan's most important exports.

Above: Irrigation channels bring life to the dry land of Al-Jazirah.

$ ECONOMY *The Gezira project*

The triangle of land between the White and Blue Niles is called 'Al-Jazirah'. It is an extremely dry area, with less than 250 millimetres of rain a year. Such areas are known as 'arid' and the only way people can support agriculture here is by artificially supplying water to the land using a process called irrigation.

In 1925 an enormous irrigation scheme was established in Al-Jazirah, by diverting the waters of the Blue Nile to the fields. Known as the Gezira project MAP REF: 1 , it is still there today. Only it is now even bigger - it covers around one million hectares, the area of 926,000 football pitches!

As we pass by the Gezira farms you will probably see farmers harvesting cotton. This is an important cash crop, that makes up almost twenty-five per cent of Sudan's exports. Sugar cane is also grown at Gezira, and taken to the giant processing factory at Kenana MAP REF: 2 in the southern part of the scheme.

NATURE *Salinisation*

You may notice that some of the fields we pass on our journey have a whitish surface. This is caused by dissolved salts and minerals left in the soil as water evaporates in the hot sun. This process is known as 'salinisation'. It has been made much worse by irrigation schemes such as Gezira.

The problem is that too much water is often used in irrigation. Instead of being absorbed by the plants and the soil, the water sits on the surface of the land and evaporates. In severe cases, over-watering can even lead to water coming to the surface as the water table beneath the soil rises. Salinisation is a huge problem for farmers. Plants cannot grow in such salty conditions, and the land can take many years to recover.

NATURE The Nile's big brother

North of Al-Jazirah, the White Nile, which we have been following, is joined by the Blue Nile. The Blue Nile is an important river in its own right. It contributes about seventy per cent of the water that eventually flows into Egypt. Let's take a short diversion from our main route and fly over the Blue Nile from its source to its confluence with the White Nile.

The Blue Nile begins life as a small stream called the Abay. This flows from a spring in the Ethiopian Highlands into Lake Tana. As we follow the river from Lake Tana we soon see the dramatic Tis Abay Falls MAP REF: 3.

The falls drop forty-five metres in a spectacular wall of furious water, which is stained brown with silt during the rains. Spray rises towards our aircraft and it is easy to see where the name Tis Abay, which means 'smoke of the Nile', came from.

For the rest of its journey, the Blue Nile and its mountain tributaries flow through deep gorges that are over 1,000 metres deep in places. It's the terrific power of the water that has cut these gorges through the surrounding landscape. As we fly above them it is not surprising to learn that some people call this area the Grand Canyon of Africa.

Above: The Tis Abay Falls are the most spectacular of all the waterfalls on the Nile.

👋 PEOPLE **A *spiritual beginning***

The small spring said to be the source of the Blue Nile holds special significance for the Ethiopian Orthodox Church, the main religion in Ethiopia. The Church believes that the water rising from a patch of marshy ground on the side of Mount Gishe is sacred and has special healing powers. Pilgrims travel great distances to visit the spring and its holy waters.

💲 ECONOMY **Using the Nile**

Ethiopia has historically used very little of the Nile's water as it flows through the country. But this is starting to change.

Rapid population growth and economic development have created more demand for water, and the government believes the Blue Nile could solve this problem.

The Ethiopian government has now built over 200 small dams. It also plans to build a much larger dam near Lake Tana that would prevent almost forty per cent of the Blue Nile's water from flowing downstream. This could severely affect the economies of Sudan and Egypt – and Egypt has already threatened to go to war with Ethiopia over the issue. Thankfully the countries sharing the Nile agreed to greater sharing of the river in a 1999 agreement called the 'Nile Basin Initiative'.

Back at Khartoum, we can see where the White Nile and the Blue Nile meet at the Nile confluence. The two rivers have very different characteristics.

The White Nile has an almost constant flow. Its waters are regulated by the sponge-like effects of the Sudd wetlands. The Blue Nile, in contrast, has a definite flood season between July and October. At that time, heavy rainfall in the Ethiopian Highlands causes the river to swell rapidly. By the time it reaches Khartoum, the Blue Nile is often over three metres higher than normal. In 1998 the river rose by sixteen metres causing widespread damage.

The power of this flood surge is so great that the weaker White Nile is forced backwards. It forms a temporary lake until the flood peak has passed. The Blue Nile floods were the main cause of the annual flooding of the Nile Valley in Egypt, but they are now controlled by a dam at Aswan.

An interesting fact about the Nile confluence is that the land between the two rivers gives Khartoum its name. It means 'elephant's trunk' and refers to the shape of the land.

Below: The Blue Nile (the narrow river) joins the White Nile (the wide river) at Khartoum. During the flood season, the waters of the White Nile are held back and swell to several times their width as you can see in this satellite photograph.

Whirling Dervishes

Just as the two Niles are quite different, so too are the twin cities located where they meet. Khartoum, the Sudanese capital is a busy city with modern offices, banks and hotels along its tree-lined streets. Omdurman, across the river, is older and more interesting.

As we walk through the souk, or market, we see the traders bartering as they have done for hundreds of years. The bustling and noisy atmosphere is very exciting and there is much to see.

Before the end of the day we visit the Hamed an-Niel mosque. Here, on a Friday evening before sunset, Sufi Muslims spin round as they dance and chant in prayer.

Above: A colourful cloth store in the hustle and bustle of an Omdurman souk.

Left: A Whirling Dervish is a captivating sight as he spins faster and faster.

They believe the spinning brings them closer to God, and it has earned them the name 'Whirling Dervishes'. It is a spectacular sight, and a reminder that, from here onwards, most of the people we will meet follow the religion of Islam.

HISTORY *The slave trade*

Though not obvious today, Khartoum was once the centre of a large slave trade. Traders captured slaves from southern Sudan and brought them to Khartoum, where they were sold into the Egyptian army. This trade continued until around 1860. It was then banned – first in Egypt, and then, by about 1877, in Sudan.

We catch a lift in a trade vessel heading north out of Khartoum to the first of the Nile Cataracts.

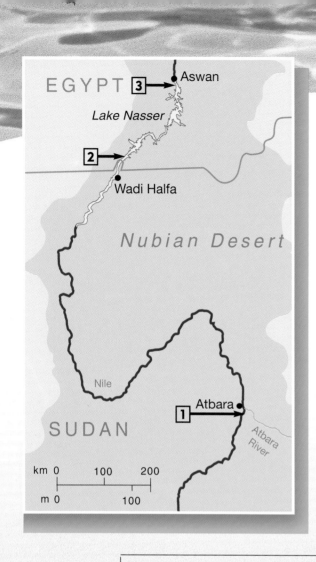

EGYPT [3] • Aswan
Lake Nasser
[2]
Wadi Halfa •

Nubian Desert

Nile

• Atbara
[1]

SUDAN

Atbara River

km 0   100   200
m 0   100

4. The Nile Cataracts

AS WE LEAVE KHARTOUM we quickly leave behind the lush swamps of southern Sudan and head into a region dominated by desert. The river is much calmer now, but its gentle flow is interrupted by several sets of rapids, called 'cataracts', where the river suddenly falls. The Nile has six cataracts and we have to travel around all of them by land, as they are too big for river traffic to navigate. Then, as we head north, you will start to notice some of the monuments that have made this part of the Nile so famous.

Below: The Nile meanders slowly through the deserts of north Khartoum. It provides a narrow ribbon of fertile land that stretches twelve kilometres on both sides of the river.

📖 **HISTORY** *The Kingdom of Kush*

About 2,700 years ago, the region between Khartoum and Aswan in southern Egypt was dominated by a Nubian civilization called the Kingdom of Kush. The Nubians shared much in common with the Ancient Egyptians.

The greatest Nubian city, and their ancient capital, was called Meroe MAP REF: 1 . Here there are many pyramids – far more than in Egypt – but the Nubian ones are not as large. The temple of Musawwarat es-Sufra is the most impressive building at Meroe. It is beautifully decorated with carved elephants. Some people have suggested that elephants may have been trained here before being sold to the Egyptians, who used them in warfare.

We know from archaeologists that the people of Meroe were skilled in making iron and gold. They also used an early water wheel called a 'saqia' to irrigate their land. There is much we don't know, however. Their alphabet, which is similar to Egyptian hieroglyphics, is not yet understood.

🐇 **NATURE** *The Nile's little brother*

At the town of Atbara we meet the last of the Nile's tributaries, the Atbara river. Like the Blue Nile, the Atbara rises in the Ethiopian Highlands and floods at around the same time of year. It contributes between ten to twenty per cent of the Nile's water. In the dry season, however, the river shrinks to a series of shallow muddy pools.

PEOPLE *The Nubians today*

No-one knows why the Nubian people lost the power they had during the Kingdom of Kush. Today they are a minority group of people, who live in the area between northern Sudan and southern Egypt.

In 1960, the construction of the Aswan High Dam in Egypt badly affected the Nubian people. Behind the dam wall, Lake Nasser flooded the Nile valley for almost 500 kilometres. The flooding forced about 90,000 Nubians to move on to higher land. Many of their historical sites and settlements were lost. But the Nubians still live close to the Nile, and most of them want to stay there.

As we travel through this region you will recognize Nubians from their long flowing clothes. The women's dress is called a 'girgar' and is worn with colourful headgear and lots of jewellery. The men wear a white floor-length robe called a 'galabia', which keeps them cool in the baking desert sun.

Perhaps we should borrow some Nubian clothes as we head into the hottest part of our journey!

NATURE *Ships of the desert*

The camel is very important to the Nubians. It is even used in wedding ceremonies – to transport gifts to the bride's family. Camels can cope with extreme desert temperatures and the terrain. They are famous for their ability to go for seven days without water. They store it in their specially adapted bloodstream.

These qualities mean that camels have been used for transporting goods across the desert for hundreds of years, earning them a reputation as 'ships of the desert'. Let's take a short camel ride on these amazing creatures. Look out for other desert wildlife as we should get a good view.

Below: A Nubian boat-builder wears the traditional 'galabia' to keep cool. You can see some of the stages of building boats in the background.

Above: Camels can drink up to one hundred litres of water in just ten minutes!
Right: The Fennec Fox digs a burrow to escape the hottest part of the day.

Other creatures have also adapted well to life in the desert. The Fennec Fox has enormous ears, and these radiate heat to keep down the fox's body temperature. The ears also act like radar, helping the fox to locate prey such as lizards and rodents that hide in the sand. Most desert animals are nocturnal. They rest in burrows during the heat of the day, so we may not see them at all. You are most likely to see lizards darting for cover, or desert insects such as the Scarab beetle scuttling along the sand.

🐇 **NATURE** *The six cataracts*

The Nile cataracts are formed where a band of harder crystalline rocks crosses the path of the river. The erosion of softer rocks downstream causes a sudden drop in the water level. This means that river traffic cannot navigate through the cataracts. Only the second cataract is passable, because it is submerged under Lake Nasser.

📖 **HISTORY** *Abu Simbel*

As we sail across the enormous Lake Nasser, it is hard to imagine that before the construction of the Aswan High Dam this was a desert river valley.

Shortly after we cross into Egypt we reach the magnificent temple of Abu Simbel MAP REF: 2, which stands high above the lake.

The temple is a permanent reminder of life before the dam. The 3,000-year-old temple was built for the pharaoh Ramses II. It is one of the finest temples in Egypt, but it was nearly lost forever when Lake Nasser flooded the land. Thankfully the Egyptians and the international community recognized its importance and launched a rescue mission. The temple was cut into giant sections and relocated to an artificial mountain built above the new level of the lake. The artificial mountain is a real engineering feat in itself.

➡ CHANGE *Aswan High Dam*

For centuries, the Nile's annual flooding provided Egyptian farmers with water and nutrient-rich sediment to fertilize their fields. But the flooding was unpredictable. It could last for months at a time or be very slight. As Egypt's population grew and land and food became scarce, this uncertainty caused great disruption to farming and food production.

In the late 1800s the Egyptians decided to try to control the floods and provide a regular flow of water by building a dam across the river. The first dam was built at Aswan in 1902, but this was too small for the might of the Nile's water. So, in 1960, construction started on an even bigger dam,

Above: Workers installing the power plant at the Aswan High Dam in the 1960s.

the Aswan High Dam MAP REF: 3 . Located about seven kilometres upstream from the original dam, and stretching 3.6 kilometres across the Nile valley, it took 50,000 workers eleven years to build.

The Aswan High Dam has succeeded in controlling the annual floods. It provides farmers downstream from the dam with a regular supply of water. As a result, farmers can now grow crops throughout the year, and farmland in Egypt has increased by about twenty-five per cent. The dam has also had some negative impacts, as we will discover later in our journey.

Left: Date palms are one of the many crops grown along the edge of the desert thanks to the life-giving waters of the Nile. Vegetables are also grown along this fertile strip of land.

We leave our ferry near the Aswan High Dam and take a short camel trek into Aswan town. Hold on tight when the camel stands up!

5. The Nile Valley

THE GREEK HISTORIAN HERODOTUS wrote, nearly 2500 years ago, that 'Egypt is the gift of the Nile'. What he meant by this was that the Egyptian people and civilization are almost entirely dependent on the Nile and its precious water. His words could not be more true. As we enter the Nile Valley below Aswan you see this for yourselves. In fact, almost all Egyptians live in the narrow fertile strip we are now entering and the delta region that awaits us at the end of our journey. This narrow ribbon of life stretches about twelve kilometres either side of the Nile. Beyond that is the world's greatest desert – the Sahara. From our felucca we gain a real understanding of the Nile's importance as it guides us gracefully towards the teeming city of Cairo.

$ ECONOMY *Aswan*

The name Aswan comes from old Greek and Egyptian words meaning 'trade'. Trade is still important in Aswan, and the market is good for exotic spices and Nubian goods. But today Aswan is dominated by the dam.

As well as flood control, the massive structure contains a HEP station that generates around fifteen per cent of Egypt's electricity. This power has helped Aswan develop as an industrial centre – the chemical fertilizer industry is especially important. Aswan is the furthest point from which the Nile can be navigated by boat from the Mediterranean, and the last town on the railway line from Cairo. The trains are busy and overcrowded, but we board a felucca for a more relaxing passage downstream.

NATURE *Elephantine Island*

As our boatman catches the breeze in the sails of the felucca we catch sight of Elephantine Island. This is an unusual rocky outcrop in the middle of the river. Archaeologists now know it was the site of the first town at Aswan.

It is not known why it is called Elephantine Island. Many people believe it was because ivory was once traded here, and others believe the smooth, granite rocks look like elephants bathing in the Nile. Whatever the reason, it is a beautiful sight. It is also one of the few points where hard rocks rise from the ground and split the Nile river into two channels.

Left: Feluccas drift gracefully on the Nile near the town of Aswan. Feluccas have been used on the Nile for hundreds of years but are now kept mainly for tourists.
Below: Aswan is famous for its spices. Chillies, cloves, saffron and turmeric are some of those being sold on this brilliantly coloured stall.

$ ECONOMY *Tourism*

Tourism is of great importance to Egypt and the River Nile is one of its main attractions. The Nile is especially interesting to visitors because so many of Egypt's ancient monuments are located along its banks. Luxurious cruise boats carry thousands of tourists along the Nile. The boats turn popular attractions into mini-harbours during the peak season.

Tourism has become Egypt's second biggest income earner after oil, but there is another side to the story. Many of the boats are owned by big companies and have everything on board – from food and guides to souvenirs. This means that local guides, called 'dragomen', are losing their customers, and local souvenir shops, hotels and restaurants are also suffering.

Some tourists still travel independently and use local services, but as the tour boats become more popular, this problem will probably increase.

Below and right: Most tourists today experience the Nile from the luxury of a cruise ship. But to gain a real sense of the river some people take a trip with a local felucca captain.

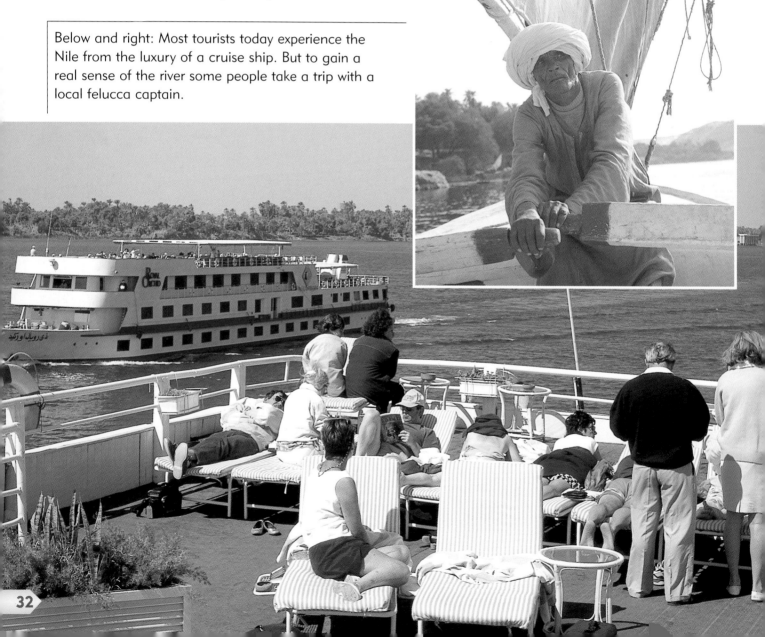

Quarrying on the **Nile**

One of the most impressive sites between Aswan and Luxor is the Temple of Horus, the falcon God, at Edfu. It is the best-preserved temple in Egypt, having been almost entirely covered by the desert until it was found in the 1860s.

In ancient times, Edfu was an important quarrying city. It was the first point coming from the north where sandstone was widely found. Sandstone was particularly valued because it was good for carving. We can see evidence of this on the giant reliefs carved into the entrance walls, or pylons, of the Temple of Horus. The temple took 180 years to build and was beautifully coloured. Today only a few painted sections remain and the paint is over 2,000 years old!

As well as being used locally, the sandstone quarried near Edfu and further south in Aswan was transported downstream by river barges and feluccas. The enormous temples at Luxor and Karnak were made with stone from the Edfu region.

Without the river, such enormous stones would have been impossible to move, and the great temples might never have been built.

Right: A dragoman, or guide, waits for tourists at the Temple of Horus, the falcon God of the ancient Egyptians. It is the most magnificent example of Ancient Egypt's monuments that visitors can see today.

PEOPLE · The Fellahin

As we sail towards Luxor you will notice farmers cultivating their fields on both sides of the River Nile. These farmers are known as 'fellahin' and live in small family groups. They grow food for themselves, and they sell anything that is left over. Some will also grow cotton or sugar as a cash crop.

One thing that you will notice about the fellahin is that some of their farming methods appear very basic. In fact they remain similar to methods used by their ancestors who farmed in the time of the pharaohs. Water is the key to success and there are several methods for lifting water

Above: The shaduf is still used by some fellahin, or farmers, to water their fields along the banks of the Nile.

from the Nile to their fields. The most simple but effective technology is a shaduf. The shaduf is a long pole with a central pivot, a weight at one end and a bucket at the other. The bucket is lowered into the water and raised again with the help of the weight at the other end. It works in much the same way as a playground seesaw. The water is then released into irrigation channels to water the crops. Modern diesel or electric pumps are replacing such traditional technology, but you may see the occasional shaduf in use.

HISTORY *Luxor*

We moor up in Luxor and explore this incredible ancient city. The enormous temples dominate the town and the riverbank, and there are often as many tourists as there are local people. On the opposite bank is the Valley of the Kings MAP REF: 1 . This hot, dusty valley is full of tombs. Here, Egyptian kings and queens were buried with their prize possessions, ready for their voyage into the afterlife.

Most of the tombs were raided hundreds of years ago and many of the treasures have been lost. But in 1922 the tomb of a young pharaoh, Tutankhamun, was discovered. It created worldwide excitement. The tomb was full of treasures and furniture that are now in the Museum of Antiquities in Cairo. Tutankhamun's fabulous gold funeral mask is one of Egypt's most famous symbols, and thousands of tourists travel here each year to visit Tutankhamun's tomb. However, not everyone is brave enough to enter. Those who unearthed the tomb suffered a series of mysterious events and accidents leading some people to believe they had been cursed by the pharaoh. Venture in if you dare, but don't say you weren't warned!

Below: The Temple of Hatshepsut and the Valley of the Kings lie beyond the sugar cane fields that line the banks of the Nile.

$ ECONOMY *Cash cropping*

As we head back to Luxor we pass two giant seated figures called the Colossi of Memnon. They are all that is left of another huge temple, looking rather strange as they sit surrounded by fields of sugar cane. Sugar cane is an important cash crop in this part of Egypt. Once the cane is cut, it is taken by tractor or donkey to be loaded on to trains for transportation to processing factories.

The growth of such cash crops is often criticized because the land could be used to grow food for Egypt's growing population instead. Cash crops are also vulnerable to changes in world prices, and farmers and their families can suffer greatly if the price suddenly falls without warning.

Despite these concerns, Egypt's production of sugar cane more than doubled from 7.5 million tonnes in 1971, to 15.7 million by 1998.

HISTORY *Early paper*

We saw papyrus growing as we passed through the Sudd region, but it is here, in Egypt, that papyrus is most famous. This tall grass once grew in abundance along the Nile and had many uses. The roots provided food and were also used as fuel and even for perfume. The stem was used for building or was split into fibres for making ropes or weaving mats. Most importantly though, papyrus provided an early form of paper, allowing written records to be easily stored and transported for the first time.

People made papyrus paper by splitting the stem into thin slices. After they were soaked in water, the slices were laid crossways, and the layers pressed together.

Below: These children are gathering cut sugar cane and loading it into railway wagons. Sugar cane is one of Egypt's most important cash crops.

Above: Papyrus paper is still made using traditional methods. Today, however, it is used mainly for tourist souvenirs.

The papyrus's gluey sap stuck the layers together as they dried in the sun. Finally the sheets were rubbed with ivory or smooth shells to give a clear writing surface.

Today papyrus is grown in special plantations, and the paper is used to make tourist souvenirs. You can see them for sale in Luxor and other popular tourist sites.

PEOPLE *Bustling riverbanks*
Our felucca leaves Luxor and we continue our journey down the Nile. Passing yet more historic sites, we enter Middle Egypt and approach the great city of Cairo. The banks become even busier as we near the most densely populated area of Egypt, and of the Nile itself. Such large numbers of people are only here because of the life the Nile brings them. There are some worrying signs, however, that the river may not be able to support so many people for much longer. Parts of the river are polluted, caused by the human actions in the region.

Below: Washing clothes in the Nile is just one source of pollution caused by people in this densely populated stretch of the Nile.

HISTORY *The Pyramids of Giza*

Before we enter Cairo we travel overland to the famous pyramids of Giza MAP REF: 2. Many people think they are the greatest wonder of the world. The pyramids are enormous burial chambers, built with individual stone blocks that were cut to precise dimensions. The biggest pyramid, Cheops, is made up of over two million blocks. It was first thought that the pyramids were built by an army of slaves.

Archaeologists now believe they were built by farmers. During the annual flooding of the Nile, farmers worked for the pharaohs in return for food, water and shelter. They returned to their fields when the floods subsided.

As you admire these extraordinary structures, it is difficult to imagine the effort it must have taken to construct them. But the task would have been even harder were it not for the Nile!

PEOPLE *A crowded city*

Arriving in Cairo is a real experience. The city is a fascinating mixture of everything ancient and everything new. International banks, offices and shopping malls line the streets of modern Cairo, while just a few

Left: The Sphinx guards the ancient pyramid of Cheops at Giza.
Below: This is the view from the top of the Cairo Tower.

Above: A crowded ferry takes people and goods across the Nile. Travelling on the river is often faster than on Cairo's congested roads.

kilometres away the narrow alleys of the 'Kahn El Khalili' souk have changed little since the fourteenth century. No matter where we go, there are people everywhere.

Cairo is one of the most populated cities in the world, with an estimated sixteen million people. One of the best ways to see this sprawling city is from the revolving restaurant at the top of the 187-metre-high Cairo Tower. Located on Gezira Island in the middle of the Nile, this famous view from the Tower gives a good idea of Cairo's size.

Going back into the city across 'el-Tahrir' bridge, you may notice people living in boats along the river. This is an indication of the city's struggle to provide for its growing population. The sight is a dramatic contrast to the five-star Hilton hotel on the bank above.

 NATURE *Air pollution*

One of the biggest problems in Cairo is traffic congestion. The noise of honking car horns around the city is deafening, but it is the fumes from all those exhaust pipes that are the real problem.

Air quality is so poor that, most days of the year, Cairo fails to meet the guidelines for safe air set down by the World Health Organisation. The pollution can give people sore throats and headaches and, in the long term, lead to more serious breathing difficulties and even cause early death.

For the final stage of our journey to the delta region we hop into a small motorized boat.

MEDITERRANEAN SEA

Alexandria
Rosetta
Damietta
Port Said
1

CAIRO

Suez

EGYPT

RED
SEA

Nile

km 0   50   100

m 0   50

6. The Nile Delta

ABOUT TWENTY KILOMETRES north of
Cairo the Nile divides into two branches.
The two channels are called the Rosetta
and the Damietta. These channels form
the Nile delta, and the area between them
is some of the most productive agricultural
land in the world. Consequently, the area is
densely populated. However, this low-lying
region is today under threat by activities
further up the Nile, and some of a much
bigger scale altogether.

Below: The Nile delta is known as the 'Rose of the
Nile'. In this satellite photograph you can see the
flower-shape at the top, and the stem stretching
back into the desert.

$ ECONOMY *The delta farms*

The Nile delta has been an important agricultural region since ancient times. It is often called 'the bread basket of Egypt'. Each year a rich layer of fertile sediment was deposited in the delta as the Nile floods fanned out over the low-lying land. Today the dam at Aswan blocks the sediment, and so farmers must rely on chemical fertilizers to improve their yields.

Flood control means the land can be farmed all year and new areas can be cultivated. Since the Aswan High Dam was built, Egypt's cultivated area has increased by over a third, mainly in the delta region.

Cotton is the most important crop grown here. Egyptian cotton is world famous for its superior quality. Rice is the other major crop, but wheat, citrus fruits, vegetables and nuts are also grown. Date palms are one of the more unusual crops. In ancient times the dates were made into a type of local wine, but today they are mainly exported as dried fruit.

⇒ CHANGE *Greening the desert*

The construction in the delta region is part of the 180-kilometre Al Salam canal and pipeline. When it is finished in 2003, the project will use water from the Damietta to irrigate the eastern delta and the deserts of northern Sinai. If it is successful, this project to 'green' the deserts of the north will increase Egypt's irrigated farmland by nearly twenty per cent. It will reduce the need for imported food and eventually allow the resettlement of 1.5 million people from the overcrowded Nile valley.

Above: Harvesting dates is a skilful task, and you need a head for heights too!

Below: Part of the Al Salam pipeline that will carry water from the Nile to irrigate new farmland in the desert.

41

Above: Fishermen often return with empty nets since the Aswan High Dam was completed.

We have travelled almost 1,000 kilometres since we left the Aswan High Dam, but the impacts of the dam are felt here in the delta more than anywhere. The loss of annual sediment deposits means that the delta is no longer building up. Instead, sections are now being eroded by the river. The delta is also retreating inland as the Mediterranean Sea swallows up large areas that are unprotected without their annual sediment deposits.

The use of chemical fertilizers has increased fourfold since the dam was completed. Large quantities of these are washed back into the Nile as 'run-off', where they pollute the water, making it saltier and less suitable for crops.

Even as far as the Mediterranean Sea, the impacts of the dam are felt. There was once a busy fishing industry near the mouth of the Nile. Fish were plentiful because they fed on the nutrients washed down by the river. The annual sardine catch was around 18,000 tonnes. Shortly after the dam was completed, catches fell dramatically and were soon down to just 500 tonnes a year. The impacts of the Aswan High Dam have taught planners to consider the whole river when they think about building dams and to carefully weigh up the benefits and costs of such projects.

$ ECONOMY   *Trade and shipping*

The delta region is at the heart of Egypt's trade and industry. Alexandria is a major industrial city, and its port handles around eighty per cent of all Egypt's imports and exports. The city and port are linked to the River Nile by a canal. This allows passenger and cargo steamers to navigate as far south as Aswan. The river is shallow through much of its course however, and during the Ethiopian and Sudanese droughts of the 1980s, the low water levels threatened the passage of some large vessels.

On the other side of the delta, Port Said is another important port. It marks the entrance to the Suez Canal, MAP REF: 1 which cuts 163 kilometres through Egypt linking the Mediterranean and Red Seas. More importantly though, the canal speeds up the journey time for ocean-going ships travelling between the Indian and Atlantic Oceans. Without the canal they would have to sail around Africa. The taxes paid by ships using the Suez Canal are an important source of income for Egypt.

Below: The Suez Canal is a vital link between Europe and Asia. Egypt earns money by charging ships for passing through the canal.

👋 PEOPLE *How many people?*

In the year 2000, the Nile basin was home to about 160 million people. If the total population of the countries sharing the Nile is included, then it was nearer 300 million. This number is likely to increase considerably in the future, because the countries of the Nile have among the fastest-growing populations in the world.

In Egypt and Sudan, which both depend heavily on the Nile, the population of 98 million in 2000 is expected to increase to 174 million by 2050. It is difficult to imagine such huge increases in this region. The settled areas are already among the most densely populated in the world. With few alternative sources of water though, it seems certain that the Nile will be the key to their future.

➡ CHANGE *Global warming*

Of all the threats and changes to the Nile we have seen on our journey, there is one that is beyond the control of the people living along its banks. Global warming, as a result of human activities altering our climate, presents a major threat to the Nile and its people.

There is evidence that rainfall in the Ethiopian Highlands has varied in recent years. This has affected the flow of the Blue Nile and the Atbara river, which provide most of the Nile's water. The pattern of rainfall is also changing, with long dry periods followed by sudden downpours. In 1998, Khartoum suffered its worst flooding in 50 years. Yet just a few years earlier it was suffering from major droughts.

Perhaps the biggest threat comes from the possibility of rising sea levels. Global warming causes the polar ice caps to melt. Many experts predict that the seas will rise by one metre by 2100. This would mean that up to thirty per cent of the low-lying Nile delta region – the area we have just visited – could be submerged. This would include much of Egypt's best farmland, as well as the important cities of Alexandria and Port Said.

Right: Much of the Nile delta could soon be flooded due to global warming. If this happens then fishing will become more important than farming for the people living in the area.

We have reached the end of our journey. We have
travelled more than 6,600 kilometres along the longest
river in the world.

The Nile continues to fascinate visitors from around
the world, although most of them see only a fraction
of what we have covered. And, although the Nile has
given up some of its secrets, it remains surrounded by
the mystery of ancient civilizations, and by the
uncertainty of its future.

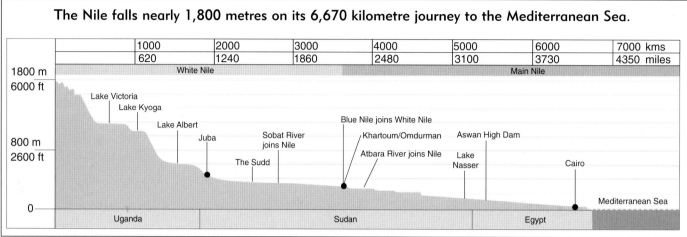

The Nile falls nearly 1,800 metres on its 6,670 kilometre journey to the Mediterranean Sea.

	1000	2000	3000	4000	5000	6000	7000 kms
	620	1240	1860	2480	3100	3730	4350 miles

White Nile — Main Nile

1800 m / 6000 ft
800 m / 2600 ft
0

Lake Victoria
Lake Kyoga
Lake Albert
Juba
The Sudd
Sobat River joins Nile
Blue Nile joins White Nile
Khartoum/Omdurman
Atbara River joins Nile
Aswan High Dam
Lake Nasser
Cairo
Mediterranean Sea

Uganda — Sudan — Egypt

Further Information

Useful websites

There are many websites that offer bits of information, but these have been chosen because they have more detail:

http://library.thinkquest.org/16645/the_land/nile_river.shtml
This website provides information about aspects of the Nile and the people living along it. It also has links to information about the cities and Lake Victoria.

http://touregypt.net/wildegypt/
This is an interesting online safari that will help you find out more about the wildlife living in and around the Nile as it flows through Egypt.

http://www.factmonster.com/ce6/world/A0835683.html
Factmonster is online information centre for young users. This address will take you directly to the Nile River entry, but use the search function to find additional information.

http://www.hewett.norfolk.sch.uk/curric/NewGeog/Africa/Nile.htm
An interesting site containing several articles about the Nile and especially the conflict over its waters between the countries sharing it – see the 'water wars' section.

Books

Great Rivers: The Nile, Michael Pollard (Evans Brothers, 2003)

Nile River (Rivers and Lakes), Cari Meister (Checkerboard Books, 2002)

Lake Victoria (Rivers and Lakes), Cari Meister (Checkerboard Books, 2002)

The Changing Face of Egypt by Ron Ragsdale (Hodder Wayland, 2002)

Themes in Geography: Rivers by Fred Martyn (Heinemann Library, 1996)

Earth Alert! Rivers by Shelagh Whiting (Hodder Wayland, 2001)

Glossary

Archaeologist A scientist who studies former human life and activity through the excavation of artefacts (things crafted by humans) and buildings.

Arid An environment in which annual rainfall is generally below 250-300 millimetres.

Cash crops Crops grown to sell for money. They include crops such as coffee, tea, sugar cane, and fruits such as apples and oranges.

Cataract A series of rapids or a waterfall.

Channel The passageway through which a river flows.

Confluence The place where two rivers meet.

Cultivating Planting, growing and harvesting crops and plants on land that has been prepared for this purpose.

Dam A barrier that holds or diverts water.

Delta A geographical feature at the mouth of a river, formed by the build-up of sediment.

Erosion The wearing away of land by natural forces such as running water, glaciers, wind or waves.

Export Products and services sold by a country to other foreign countries. For example fruit and wine sold by South Africa to European countries.

Felucca A small trading boat with triangular sails.

Flood control Measures taken to reduce flooding, for example, the building of sea walls, river barrages (barriers built across rivers) and reservoirs.

Flood peak The time during a flood when the floodwaters are at their highest.

Flood surge A sudden increase in the volume of floodwater, which creates a giant wave.

Geological faults Fractures or breaks in the rocks that form the Earth's surface or 'crust'.

Global warming The gradual warming of the Earth's atmosphere as a result of greenhouse gases trapping heat. Human activity has increased the level of greenhouse gases, such as carbon dioxide and methane, in the atmosphere.

Gorge A deep, narrow river valley with steep, rocky sides.

Headwaters Streams found at the source of a river.

Hieroglyphics Ancient Egyptian writing often found carved on the walls of Pharaohs' tombs.

Hydroelectric Power (H.E.P.) Electricity generated by water as it passes through turbines.

Import Products and services brought in from an outside country.

Irrigation The artificial application of water to crops to make up for low or unpredictable rainfall.

Pastoralists People who depend primarily on livestock (especially cattle) for their livelihoods.

Pharaoh The title given to Ancient Egyptian kings.

Quarrying The removal of stone, or other material, from an area of land (a quarry) by digging, cutting, drilling or blasting with dynamite.

Rapids Fast-moving stretches of water where white, often violent, waves form due to rocks near the river's surface.

Runoff Water that drains from the land and runs into streams or rivers. It may carry dissolved chemicals or pollution within it.

Salinisation A process in which freshwater becomes saltwater. As the saltwater evaporates, salts become highly concentrated in water and soils, which affects plant growth. In extreme cases land may be abandoned.

Sediment Fine sand and earth that is moved and left by water, wind or ice.

Shaduf A traditional machine used to raise water from a channel, made up of a bucket, rod and pivot.

Source The point at which a river begins.

Subsistence farming Farming that provides food mainly for the household. Surplus food may be sold.

Terrain An area of land.

Thatching A skilled process whereby roofs are constructed or tightly covered with plant materials, such as straw or reeds.

Tributary A stream or river that flows into another larger stream or river.

Turbines Machines consisting of rotor blades that turn under the force of moving water and generate electricity.

Vessels Ship, boats or rafts used to transport goods or people.

Waterfall A sudden fall of water over a steep drop.

Index

Abu Simbel 28
Alexandria 43
Al Salam canal and pipeline 41
animals 13, 15, 16, 26, 27
Aswan 31
Aswan High Dam 26, 28-29, 31, 41, 42
Atbara river 25, 44

Basoga people 11
Blue Nile 18, 19, 20, 21, 22, 44
boats (see also felucca) 5, 9, 26, 32, 39
Bujagali Falls 8
Burton, Richard 7

Cairo 37, 38, 39
camels 26, 27, 29
cash crops 34, 36
cattle 15
cotton 18, 19, 34, 41
crops 11, 34, 36, 41

dams 8, 9, 21, 26, 28, 29, 31, 41
date palms 29, 41
Dinka 14, 15, 17

Edfu 33
Elephantine Island 31
Ethiopian Highlands 20, 22, 44
Ethiopian Orthodox Church 21

farmers and farming 11, 13, 19, 28, 29, 34, 36, 38, 41
felucca 30, 31, 32
fishing 10, 11, 14, 15, 42
floods 16, 22, 25, 26, 28, 29, 38, 41, 44

Gezira project 19
global warming 44

hydroelectric power 8, 31

industry 31
irrigation 19, 25, 34

Jonglei Canal 17

Khartoum 22, 23, 24, 44
Kush, the Kingdom of 25, 26

Lake Nasser 26, 28
Lake Victoria 5, 6, 7, 10, 11
Luxor 35

Meroe 25
Murchison Falls 12, 13

national parks 13
Nile cataracts 24, 28
Nile delta 40, 41, 44
Nubians 25, 26

Omdurman 23
Owen Falls Dam 8, 10

papyrus 36, 37
pollution 37, 39, 42
population growth 11, 21, 44
Port Said 43
pyramids 25, 38

quarrying 33

Rift Valley 12
Ripon Falls 6, 7, 8

salinisation 19
shaduf 34
shipping 43
slave trade 23
source, Nile's 7
Speke, John Hannington 7
Sudd wetlands 16, 17, 22
Suez Canal 43
sugar cane 19, 35, 36

Temple of Horus 33
Tis Abay Falls 20, 21
tourists and tourism 13, 32, 35, 37
trade 31, 43
Tutankhamun 35

Valley of the Kings 35

water hyacinth 10
White Nile 6, 18, 20, 22
wildlife (see also animals) 13